ENLIGHTENED LOVE

ENLIGHTENED LOVE

Poetry For The Soul

Stephen Mulhearn

Giant Steps

This edition published in Great Britain in 1998 by
Giant Steps
65 Livingstone Park
Kilsyth
Glasgow G65 9NT
Tel: 0374 263 544

ISBN 0-9532995-0-3

British Library Cataloguing - in - Publication Data.
A catalogue record for this book is
available from the British Library.

Designed and printed by:-
Cowan Print
6-8 Market Square
Kilsyth G65 0AZ

Cover illustration and sketches
by Australian Artist Pilar Stewart.

Dedicated to everyone who
gave me permission to shine!

Most of all, for my family, Edith,
Martin, Margaret Anne, Frank and Martin.

Since the conception of life began, we have searched for our true purpose.

Enlightened Love transcends beyond the human body and crosses the bridge to spiritual bliss.

Believe in your spiritual soul and it will be your guide.

Acknowledge your wings, and prepare for the greatest adventure of all.

The journey to the throne of your soul.

Bags of knowledge
carry too much weight
to enjoy the lightness
of wisdom.

Love is never jealous
it bathes in kindness.
Love is never restrictive
it flows unconditionally.
Love is not a gift
it is a birthright.
Love never dies
it chooses to be reborn.

As the last hand waved to 12 o'clock
evening modelled a funeral frock.
Little boys and little girls
swam in dreams of mystic worlds.
Bells did toll across the land
as blood thrust into the veins
of Satan's hands.

Slowly his eyes did open
the clouds did part.
The moon penetrated night to
glorify the dark.
Nick's lips did moisten
for the menu of fear.

A La Carte more expensive
takes longer to prepare.
Oh please Oh please
put away the cutlery,
one's nails more sharpened
and willing to tear.

When the deed was done
Darkness did retreat.
The flickering eyelids
of street lights slept
as daylight engulfed
the blood soaked street.
The soul of the body danced
up through the air,
a figure arrived,
so innocent and fair.

An angel from heaven sent to collect
the contents of a container
intact from the wreck.
Gently the angel caught the soul,
and wrapped it in virgin white wings
to protect from the cold.

With haste and purpose they
sped through the sky
to a blood soaked table
where a woman did lie.
Into her womb the soul was placed
a last push of pain she then did embrace.

As her muscles relaxed
 and oxygen was given.
A child was born
and Satan forgiven.

FOR WHAT YOU THOUGHT

No more swimming freely
no more running fast.
What you hoped for love
what you thought was love,
come back days of past.
I saw it in the summer nights
I thought it was yet to come.
My fingers ran through it slightly
my senses tamed
to the unintelligent days of fun.

Good days are lost
my soul now weeps,
oh that of those who didn't have to cry
would manage to touch passing shadows,
gently then whisper goodbye.

Seek the path
that leads to your inner love
then spend eternity
giving it to all that is.

The poet proclaimed "love is mine to behold,"
enjoy it, as you read my works of art
but the blind could not see this work of art.
Then the musician drew harmony from the harp
and announced "my music is the secret of love,"
but the deaf could not hear this secret of love.
Then the holy man rose to his feet and preached,
"tell me your sins, and in return I'll bless
you with love," but those without speech
could not receive this blessing.
Then a mother lifted her child
and gently entwined their hearts in an embrace.
An infinity of love blossomed so brightly
that feelings of joy shone in every soul.

As a boy I dreamt of becoming a man
as a man I played as a child.
Confused I searched for enlightenment
enlightened I drew darkness from the confuse
For love I looked into every heart
in my own soul I found my other half.

For riches I built my own company
from the company of others
I found a wealth of love.
To receive anything that
my soul had need for
I gave that which I desired
to everyone I met.
By learning through experience
I was taught everything I already knew.

In regards of my boyhood dream
of saving the world,
I have taken sail on the ripples
 belonging to the pond of life.
Concerning my search for
the meaning of life
my gift to all is compassion and love.

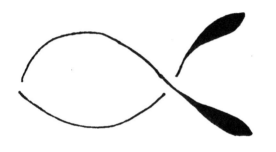

INFINITY OF THE HUMAN SPIRIT

Though towering walls shall crumble,
and mighty rocks will be split open
by the flowing river,
honesty shall stand strong.
As autumn's winds blow north
and forests are stripped naked,
green leaves retreat, as their soft skin
withers to brown and their fragile beauty
cracks, and is cast forth into the skies,
yet dignity shall stand strong.

Whilst kings are trapped
by the possessions of wealth
and wars are waged against the meek,
screaming children stand witness
to the self righteous slaughter of innocent beliefs,
yet compassion shall stand strong.
Eyes diluted by tears of the heart
overflow with loss,
as our mother's and father's
spirits trickle gently back into the earth
leaving fond memories to be
played from time to time,
yet love shall stand strong.

When the illusion of loneliness
cloaks our hearts
and true friends are hard to find,
abandoned values are traded
for cold comforts
as dreams are scattered beyond
retrievable reach
still faith shall stand strong.

Though we can be stripped of possessions,
our securities and companions,
our human spirit of resolve
shall stand strong.

People don't stop loving
each other
they simply stop
giving each other
permission to feel love.

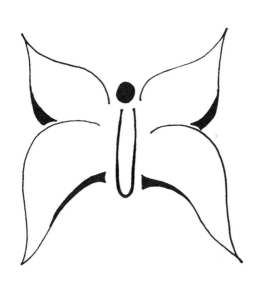

LOVE IS A CHOICE NOT A GIFT

What is it that separates the dreamer
from his mirror reflection of consciousness?
How can one man expire to a state of ecsta
whilst his brother cries himself to sleep?
If we can create our own destiny
then surely destiny is a simple piece of clay
moulded in the shape and texture of its
masters hands.
Every curve and shadow cast by
the unborn creation
carries the fingerprints and sweat,
the pain and anxieties,
of a thousand movements.

Every action must have, and will
have a counter action.
Nature by its very nature in
its most primitive self
casts a life giving, life growing
deliverance of pure light
replacing darkness in its wake.
Lifting the tender necks of sleeping flowers
releasing from safety and confinement
the pollen of the future
history of the coming rebirth.

Creating tomorrow's breathtaking gardens
of vibrant colours that an artist
by his name itself would cherish
on his palette
Potent with perfumed air
to caress the senses of every child and
offspring that screamed with joy
in celebration of the release of
their evolution and birth.

These gardens mirror the
sound of silence found only in
the tranquillity of the peaceful soul.
At one with nature in a
pure state of abstraction,
from the body of its shell.

To touch the innocence and
smoothness of these petals
send trickles of pure happiness,
and love to all.
Unbiased in its flow,
to the fingertips of a convict
in a caged prison yard,
or to the holy man at
peace in God's courtyard.

Why is it then that the mysterious woman
who sits quietly on the same bench,
in the same park,
round about the same
time every Friday
will fill her tender senses with the
joys and love that natural beauty
gives freely and unconditionally to
every living creation of this earth?

At the same time as her young
upwardly manipulative partner
only a thought away
bulldozes through a forest of
timeless love and beauty
that mother nature herself did dream
a thousand years ago.

To make way for progress
and the construction of
a new hitech coffin box
they call the future.
To house workers under
man-made lights that know not
the changes of the seasons
or even the birth of dawn.

What is it that separates the dreamers
and gives the energy of love to their lives?
They simply choose to give water to the plant,
firstly to give life and love that blossoms flowers,
and secondly to receive the beauty and joy
that every open petal releases,
in return for the emotion we call love.

THE JOURNEY

This is my last life on earth
I'm going to miss it.
So many special moments,
so many special friends
unbreakable bonds entwined in love.
I'm going to miss it.

This last trip shall be the
mother of them all
the final contribution,
before I become one.
Life-force carries my every thought
it delivers all my supplies,
for my finale and most
everlasting adventure.
Mother earth has given
me so much love
I'm going to miss it.

My feelings are of both
relief and excitement.
My most significant gift
to the world is yet to come.
I'm so grateful and privileged,
to have been chosen for
such a magical chore,
earth has granted me so
much joy and happiness.
I'm going to miss it.

On my last few seconds of this life
I shall carve the words "thank you"
as I transcend to a state of infinity.
I shall rejoice in the raptures of love,
and send a smile across a dawning sunrise.

A state of grace shall ripple through every anir
and war will indeed be extinct.
May all who read this
walk barefoot on mother earth
it is true, it does tickle her back.
I'm going to miss it.

Your eyes open the gateway of my soul,
those lips whisper verses that are melodious to my ears,
You complete me.
Your fingertips are the keys that scale the heights of my
spinal cord, as your hot breath erects the hairs on
the back of my neck,
You complete me.
Bathing with you, cleanses my darkest thoughts
and moistens my well travelled skin,
You complete me.
Being inside you, makes the ripened juices of my cup
overflow,
as I taste the sweetness of your pleasures.
You complete me.
As we dance naked, around a mighty fire
in the forest break,
your sweating body basks in the light of the full moon,
as your impure sexual desires are legalised.
Feast on my flesh, drink the fruitful wines of my soul.
Take the offering of my seed,
and mother it in your womb.
You make me pant like a bitch in heat.
You make me cry, tears of joy.
You make me an adventurous child again.
You teach me new chapters of love.
You complete me.

I am a teacher
whose lifelong class is on love.
I am a farmer
who reaps a harvest of souls.
I am a servant who
obeys the master of my dreams.
I am a student
who learns through my own disharmony.
I am a garden who needs
your compassion for growth.
I am the voice that
whispers to you in silence.
I am your brother and sister
and all that you can be.
To see my face with all its
angelic beauty, step up to a mirror
and smile.
Behold with grace
the beauty of your spirit
For you are a teacher
whose lifelong class is on love.

My love crumbles the pillars of loneliness
with the healing power of hope.
For I have found my true path to follow,
which leads to a place of warm safety,
and an abundance of summer meadows,
ablaze with golden fields
of timeless daydreams.

I pray with pure soul, to all that is sacred,
that my wishes be blessed by an angel.
An angel with white feathered leaves of grace
for her back.
And an autumn evening of clear skies
glittering with an audience of distant stars
for her halo.

To picture her lips,
is to stand before the gates of nirvana.
Now lift your vision to her eyes,
that reflect a new morning sun
with as much beauty and awe
as one's first sight of a Pacific sunset.

To touch the fragile beauty of her skin
sends rushes up my spine and
makes me tremble like an excited child.
Were I to be a martyr, then her footprints
 would guide me on my way.
I would without hesitation carry a crucifix
of thirst, if only to know
that my sacrifice rained life
onto the petals of her wild flower.

When this shrine to female beauty speaks,
my ears fall deaf to all but her words.
For I choose to be her obedient slave.
If defiant love be a sinner
then cast me deep into the flames of her hea
and may the power of my thoughts
beam an almighty light, towards
the prism of her love.
To be dispersed through her glory
and channelled to all corners of the universe
like a rainbow crossing the bridge of time.

For to love her is to love all.
She is my guiding dolphin,
my country of pride,
and my orchard of heaven's paradise.
As much as I would gladly lay down
my life for her,
I would greater prefer to live for eternity
by her side.
You see, this angel is my teacher,
who tunes my soul.
Her fingertips pluck
unwelcome thoughts
from my fields of dreams
and her compassion has already
answered my every prayer.
If love be a religion,
then I have found my God.

To the temple I bring my gift,
I place my offering unconditionally,
I require no thank you
nor do I expect a token in return.
Tomorrow I shall again deliver my gift,
once more, no receipt is asked for.
The day after tomorrow I shall
retrace my steps
and return yet again to place my offering
at the feet of the altar.
Everyday thereafter my pilgrimage shall shine
with unconditional faith.
This act requires no significance from others,
its quest is performed in meditated silence.
My religion is love.
My temple is the universe.
My prayer is the verse of giving.
My altar is your heart.
My state is gratitude.
My gift is forgiveness.
My purpose is to channel light.
My hope is that your voice joins
 this spiritual silence.
My love........is already yours.

Let your love flow
so that it may travel.
Give freedom to your soul,
that it may be exalted.
Touch others with a gentle forgiveness
and release light from their infinite star.
Go on a date with mother nature
and return with fruitful gifts of love for
your brothers and sisters.
Never build barricades to constrict your love
or disharmony shall follow.
Share joy and beauty with all at your table,
for in giving we are truly released
to channel heavenly love.
Be at peace now, you are a child of the unive
and remember, heaven always was on earth.
From this day forth light a candle, that others
may find their own way home.

Let us begin our story on page one
your spirit has chosen your parents wisely
and the conception of your destiny has begun.
The seeds of two hearts now
working day and night
to sew together a human temple,
a tapestry of flesh and blood,
rehearsed for nine months,
in preparation for your spirits flight.
As the curtain rises, the audience
screams with joy,
your new body takes centre stage
and a choir of angels sing with delight
in celebration of this new arrival to Troy.

Your warm up, of many lives
has prepared you to take your place,
at the starting blocks of a divine journey
called the human race.
As your mind mentally focuses
on your destination,
and your chosen way.
A voice from your future history
whispers "carpe diem"
to remind you to cherish magic moments
on each and every day.

All of a sudden shadows flicker around you,
giving the cue that the game has already begun
but which way do you choose?
Blind panic surrounds,
as bodies sprint in every direction
no one seems to know their destination,
close your eyes child, and take direction
from your innerself
as the voice calmly announces,
"with haste my prodigy, head for the sun."

Like a tiger unleashed from a cage
your spirit powers down a rarely travelled path,
tossing obstacles adrift to the seas of doubt
for hesitant others to collect and
add to the weight of their self created, sinking raf
As your novel unfolds along the way
you temporarily feel cloaked in darkness,
as you arrive at the necessary
stage known as writer's block.
So you centre your being in the
heart of solitude's silence
as your inner guide delivers the clues needed
to help you cast aside
the illusion of immovable rocks.

Day by day your character becomes
a messenger of love, delivering gifts
of compassion and forgiveness to all.
Whilst your spirit gathers volunteers
and rages battle against your
self constructed walls.
As your final pages unfold,
and your contribution is almost complete.
You add your chapter to the book of life
and prepare to join the other captains,
on deck of thine admiral's fleet.

Your life's mission has been a legacy,
a guiding inspiration to all.
The world will remember your
regaining your stance
after each and every fall.
Step up once more, and join with your God
as your spirits evolution shines bright,
the curtain is ready to rise
in celebration of the birth
of another glorious opening night.
What is the name of this wondrous play
the programme for this evening
is "seize the day."

As man is created in the image of infinite love
so then he must be reminded of suffering,
for in that place, we learn to appreciate beauty,
the beauty of the spiritual being
dwelling in our soul.
The winters of our discord,
prepare the soil of our destiny
for new seeds. And from the youth
of these seeds, mature ripened
opportunities of reality.

Be conscious of the garden of life,
because where there is flower, there is weed
and this never ending battle
is called growth.
Forthwith, in your being,
when you taste the bitterness
of disharmony,
remember you are the only
gardener in the forest of your life.

You alone have the power and skills
to weed out unwelcome roots, as you
also have the hands to shape a
garden of paradise.
Once we master our own given plot,
we must scale the heights
of our limiting fence and share our
skills unconditionally with
our neighbours, regardless of the
condition of their fields.

As we cast forth our knowledge and love,
our own garden will govern
itself wonderfully.
Stand tall and behold this land
you have created,
for your labours of giving have
blossomed tenfold,
and your summers shall be glorious

INCANTATION OF HEALING

"Every part of my being is abundant in perfect
health. The infinite power of the universe
flows through me, cleansing and purifying my
body and mind. The infinite healing
presence within me transforms
every cell of my being
creating perfect health now and always."

ABOUT THE AUTHOR

ephen Mulhearn is a successful inspirational speaker
ho coaches clients to new levels of abundance in their
es.

s company Giant Steps, based in Glasgow, has
ntributed to people from all walks of life. His seminars
omise to deliver the tools necessary to shape a more
filling destiny.

ephen coaches clients to new levels of abundance
notionally, mentally, spiritually, physically and
ancially, as well as encouraging the seeds of greater
ationships.

find out more about the author, Giant Steps seminars,
ditation retreats, Stephen's forthcoming novel and
ur personal launch invite, or to simply give the author
ur feelings of his book, please call or write to:

Giant Steps
65 Livingstone Park,
Kilsyth,
Glasgow G65 9NT
Tel: 0374 263 544

BIG THANK YOU'S

To Emma Gray for her belief in my writings, Paul McGraine for not letting me off the hook, Andy Cartlidge and Danny Whittle for joining me in the celebration of life, Pilar Stewart for her beautiful art and companionship in Hawaii, Richie Sheeran for his music, friendship and total laughs , Craig Cowan for his honesty, support and free wheelin sense of humour, Tony Robbins for helping me discover my own wings and to every spirit who inspired me to put crayon to paper.

Finally to the tribe;

Julie, Andy, Lorraine, Davie, Kate, Gerry, Paul, Mark, John, Henry, John, Doxy, Kenneth, Babs, Marion, Fiona, Emma and all the rest ....shine on.

I truly hope that my book has given you pleasure. Believe in yourself and pursue your dreams defiantly. Hope to meet you in person some day soon. Stephen.